To: _____

From: _____

Other books by Gregory E. Lang:

Why a Daughter Needs a Mom
Why a Daughter Needs a Dad
Why a Son Needs a Mom
Why a Son Needs a Dad
Why I Love Grandma
Why I Love Grandpa
Why I Chose You
Why I Love You
Why I Still Love You
Why I Need You
Why We Are a Family
Why We Are Friends
Brothers and Sisters
Sisters
Simple Acts
Love Signs
Life Maps
Thank You, Mom
Thank You, Dad
Because You Are My Son

Because You Are My Daughter...

WHAT I HOPE YOU NEVER FORGET

GREGORY E. LANG

CUMBERLAND HOUSE

Published by Cumberland House Publishing, an imprint of Sourcebooks, Inc.
P.O. Box 4410, Naperville, Illinois 60567-4410
(630) 961-3900
Fax: (630) 961-2168
www.sourcebooks.com

Printed and bound in the United States of America.
LB 10 9 8 7 6 5 4 3 2 1

To Meagan and Linley, with a whole lotta love

Place a personal photograph here.

Include a personal note here.

INTRODUCTION

I wrote my first book, *Why a Daughter Needs a Dad*, nearly a dozen years ago. It was originally a letter really, a missive to who was then my only child, reassuring her of my love and commitment to being the best dad I could possibly be. She was only eight years old at the time but regardless of her young age, I wanted her to know, and have a lasting reminder of, just how much she meant to me and what kind of father I wanted to be for her. In that book I shared my hopes and dreams about what her future might hold and what role I would play in that future.

During the ensuing years I have reflected on that book and wondered about how well I've lived up to the expectations I created when I put my thoughts and feelings on paper. I think I've done rather well on many measures, but I also must admit to having failed on numerous others. Indeed, there have been shrieks of joy and tears of laughter in my home (now inhabited by two daughters) occurring right alongside wind-sucking sobs and outbursts born of bitter disappointment. I've made as many child-rearing mistakes as any parent and often find myself envious of other parents who I believe handled a certain situation or dilemma far better than I did or might have.

Yet in spite of my parenting missteps and the occasional "I don't have a clue about what to do now" quandary, I continue to desire as much as anything else to be the best parent I can possibly be. As any parent knows, the happiness and well-being of your own child is the highest achievement you can hope for. No matter how often we may blunder as parents, or how often we face disappointments, nothing quenches our love for our children, extinguishes our desire to see them thrive and prosper, or thwarts our ambition to have a meaningful role in their lives.

That is why we parents do what we do: save baby teeth and locks of hair, tempera-paint masterpieces and yellowed report cards; attend every recital, spelling bee, and sporting event we can cram into our schedules; wait sleeplessly for teens to come home; fall asleep praying for wisdom and miracles; cry at high school graduations; and do everything we can to postpone our children's eventual departure from home. Because it is our children who give us something that cannot be obtained from any other source—a sense of place in a life that is more important than your own, the life of your child.

And now all these years later, years of saving, watching, waiting, and praying, years which have, by the way, produced a rich tapestry of memories to comfort me when it seems I'm left behind as the girls get on with their own budding lives, I still have high hopes and big dreams for my daughter and step-daughter. And I continue to want each to know just how much they mean to me.

So herein I return to a frame of mind and place in my heart where I found myself over a decade ago as I sat down to write a simple letter. Older, wiser, slower perhaps, but one thing surely remains the same—I love my girls with all my heart. In fact, they are my heart, and I want to tell them why...

May your father and mother always be glad,
and may you always give them reason to rejoice.

Because
You Are
My Daughter...

*Because you are
my daughter...*

I've loved you from the moment

our eyes first met.

The most beautiful face in the world

has always been yours.

You may not remember everything, but

*because you are
my daughter...*

I remember it all:

your sweet baby's breath,

your excitement to see me,

your warm hugs all the day long.

Your tiny hand in mine.

The sound of your little feet

running across the floor.

Your bubbly voice calling my name,

and every good-night kiss you gave.

You are my daughter,

all filled with wonder.

You marveled when flowers bloomed

and butterflies took wing.

You sat on my shoulders,

reached for the sky,

and counted all the stars in heaven.

We danced in the kitchen

and jumped on the bed;

we shared ice cream in the sun

and sang the same silly songs over

and over again.

You are my daughter...

you reminded me to play and have fun,

and taught me to use my imagination again.

Because of you I believe in Santa

and the Tooth Fairy once more.

I loved caring for your cuts and bruises

and being the one who caught you

just before your falls.

You let me be there when you encountered

life's little challenges,

and you encouraged me as you listened to

what I wanted to teach you.

You filled my life with that

special something I'd been missing,

and you've enriched my life

in more ways than I can count.

You are my daughter,

and when you found your place in the world,

I found mine: being the parent you needed.

I've loved that innocent smile on your face

and most of your brave and zany ways.

I love sharing in your good times

and am grateful when you turn to me

in your bad times.

You've added immeasurable joy to my life.

You've indulged me

when I wanted to hold you forever,

you always soaked in the love

I had to give you,

and you gave me your love

without hesitation.

You are always first in my prayers.

*Because you are
my daughter,*

you are my heart.

You've made me feel as if

I'm the luckiest parent in the world.

Watching you grow up

has been a blessing to me,

and no matter how much you've grown

and changed,

our loving bond has remained

strong and true.

You have been an endless source of

comfort and support;

you never hesitate to help me

when I am tired or overwhelmed.

*Because you are
my daughter,*

you remind me to slow down, relax,

and enjoy the day with you.

You've been forgiving when

I was frustrated and impatient.

You always seem to know

how to get me in a better mood,

and you remind me

not to take myself so seriously.

You've kept me in a youthful state of mind

and pushed me to adapt with a

changing world.

———————

I've learned so much along the way

and relish the adventure of

keeping up with you.

You've brought new rewards into my life

and caused me to shed a few bad habits.

Together we've made

important discoveries

and sorted out what once

kept us awake.

*Because you are
my daughter,*

we bring out the best in each other,

and sometimes I can see a

little bit of me in you.

We both like hazelnut cream

in our coffee

and peanut butter on our pretzels.

———

We can chat for hours and

never get bored,

and sometimes we just sit,

say nothing at all…

and are happy together nonetheless.

Yet in ways we are different

from one another,

and those differences can

frustrate us both.

But our frustrations are never permanent.

Nothing can come between us.

*Because you are
my daughter,*

I brag about your accomplishments.

You'll never be too old for me

to cheer you on;

though it may embarrass you,

I just can't help it.

———

My delight in you never fades.

The love between us continues to grow,

and although the years have changed us,

our relationship remains as strong as ever.

We love the comfort of togetherness,

yet respect each other's private

time and space.

———————

As life has taken us our separate ways,

you've shown me you still need me.

When I miss you I read all the cards

and letters you've ever given me,

and each one reminds me that

it is important to you, too,

that we never lose touch with

each other.

You give me time when I call to say "I miss you,"

and now and then you call me to say that too.

No matter how long our separation,

we always pick up where we left off.

You never seem to tire of my old stories,

and I'm always thrilled to hear of your

new passions and interests.

You never have so much to do that

you can't stop and have a little fun with me,

and you remind me I'm never too old to play

like we once used to.

I'm so proud of who you've become,

and I'm so hopeful about where you are going.

Wherever you end up, one thing will be sure—

I'll be proud of you there and then too.

You have shared your heart and

your dreams with me,

and your dreams have become mine.

*Because you are
my daughter,*

in my heart and dreams you will always be.

ACKNOWLEDGMENTS

Thank you, God, for without your blessing my writings would still be in a shoe box in the dark recesses of my closet. My words are yours; I am merely the hand that puts them on paper. To you goes the Glory!

Behind every good book is a great team, and that is certainly the case with this book. I have also been blessed with the love and support, creative inspiration, and good old-fashioned dogged determination of many people who have guided my writing through the transition from words scrawled on paper to a hardback book on a bookstore shelf. With that truth in mind, I'd like to give a heartfelt thanks to the following people:

My dear wife, Jill, who encourages me more than anyone, who has unabashed faith in my person, and who doesn't scold me too harshly as she redlines every spelling, grammar, and structural error in my rough drafts. She contributes far more to my success than she gets credit for. I love her beyond measure; she is my best friend.

The young daughters in my life, Meagan Lang and Linley Davis. Without their love, affection, and kind indulgence of my habit of sharing with the world the details of their lives, this book could not have been written. My fond memories of my two sweethearts will remain with me always.

All my new friends at Sourcebooks, Inc., who did a stellar job turning my vague idea into this book. In particular, I'd like to thank

Dominique Raccah who believed in my talent and chose to give me a new platform for expressing myself, Peter Lynch for advocating for me, and Sara Kase, my editor, for bringing my vision to a beautiful reality. I'm so pleased to be in a new publishing home, and I look forward to our mutually rewarding future.

My family, friends, neighbors, and even a few strangers who remained patient with me as I posed, reposed, and posed them again in a vain effort to capture the perfect photographs to illustrate this book. I thank you all for being the faces to accompany these words.

And finally I wish to thank my parents, Gene and Dianne Lang, who have been my best teachers of all things about parenting during the last fifty years. Thinking about how they managed to do so much for their five children over all these years still drops my jaw.

To Contact the Author

Write in care of the publisher:
Gregory E. Lang
c/o Sourcebooks, Inc.
P. O. Box 4410
Naperville, IL 60567-4410

Email the author or visit his website:
gregoryelang@gmail.com
www.gregoryelang.com